FORREST S. CUCH
MICHAEL CARNEY

# A NATIVE WAY OF GIVING

A little book
on faith &
money

Morehouse Publishing
NEW YORK

Unless otherwise noted, the Scripture quotations contained herein are from the New Revised Standard Version Bible, copyright © 1989 by the Division of Christian Education of the National Council of Churches of Christ in the United States of America. Used by permission. All rights reserved worldwide.

Church Publishing Incorporated
19 East 34th Street
New York, NY 10016

Cover design by Jennifer Kopec, 2 Pug Design
Typeset by Progressive Publishing Services

Library of Congress Cataloging-in-Publication Data
A record of this book is available from the Library of Congress.

ISBN-13: 978-1-64065-439-6 (paperback)
ISBN-13: 978-1-64065-440-2 (ebook)

# Contents

# Introduction

This book took shape in conversations at our kitchen tables over the five years we've known each other. Forrest had left his Roman Catholic roots to find a new home at St. Elizabeth's Episcopal Church in Whiterocks, Utah, where he didn't have to sacrifice his values to be part of a faith community. Michael had been called to serve as a priest in that congregation and was learning to minister in a Native (Indigenous) community. We quickly recognized each other as kindred spirits, though our life's journeys were very different.

Forrest grew up as a member of the Ute Indian Tribe on the Uintah and Ouray Ute Reservation in northeast Utah, and he crossed many boundaries in graduating from two of Utah's most prestigious institutions: Wasatch Academy and Westminster College. After serving for years as a tribal executive back home and in Massachusetts, he was Utah's Director of Indian Affairs under four governors. He proved to be a uniquely gifted bridge person, advocating for the needs of Native people while helping them adapt to the harsh realities of the dominant culture. His spirituality incorporates Christian worship and theology alongside Native traditions like the sweat lodge and Sun Dance.

After being born and raised in Iowa, Michael's life opened up in his twenties as he explored the West, discovering a love of hiking, gardening, and teaching. After a long absence from church, he and his wife were drawn back into a small-town congregation dedicated to worship and serving the community. Ordained ministry found him serving as a pastor to West African Episcopalians (many of them refugees) and working with a group of colleagues to establish a regional youth program focused on community service. A surprising act of the Holy Spirit led to him being called to serve on the Ute reservation at St. Elizabeth's, where he has taken special delight in helping Native leaders build up their arts program for children and youth.

Despite the differences in our backgrounds we find many strong connections, and our conversations have developed into wide-ranging explorations of our faith, our families, and the perilous state of the world. We begin this writing with urgent questions in our hearts. In the face of environmental devastation, are mainstream Americans willing to adapt and make meaningful changes? Is spiritual and economic transformation possible in today's polarized environment? With the global pandemic as a catalyst, could this be the time when we respond in meaningful ways to the crises we're facing?

If so, traditional Native values and practices offer new ways of seeing our world and living in it together. Despite a grim history of violence, seizure of lands, and cultural destruction, Native communities have gifts to offer that are desperately needed. The life-giving cycle of gratitude, generosity, and abundance stands in stark contrast to the arrogance, greed, and destruction that are so widespread in modern-day life. Our experiences of crossing cultural boundaries and adapting to new challenges give us hope that change is possible, but we know it won't be easy. Still, the Spirit is crying out to us to find a better way forward for all of our people.

We're deeply grateful for the opportunity to share these thoughts and stories, especially to the bishop of Utah, The Right Rev. Scott Hayashi, and to our editor at Church Publishing, Nancy Bryan. We're thankful for our families, for the people who helped to shape our paths, and for the friends who have encouraged us along the way. Most of all we give thanks to the Creator, Jesus, and the Spirit, for their presence with us and the hope they give us for the future.

# 1 ▪ Cycles of Life

We're living in a world that is out of balance. Some people have plenty, but most have too little. Those with the greatest power and influence seem to have lost touch with the Creator and lost respect for creation. For us to survive, a time of cleansing and renewal is urgently needed.

The challenge of transforming a world that has lost its balance begins with trying to understand what a more harmonious state would be like. White folks like me (Michael) can learn from the wisdom of Native people, who for thousands of years have been observing and celebrating the cycles of nature. The contrasts of day and night and the changing of the seasons are two obvious examples. Here are some others: the respiration of plants and animals exchanges oxygen and carbon dioxide, keeping the atmosphere in balance. Leaves drop from trees in autumn to enrich the soil that will feed their roots the next spring. Rain falls and is carried by rivers back to the ocean, from which new rain clouds are formed by the sun.

Native people have related observations like these to their own life cycles. For example, the burial and decomposition of their bodies nourishes the soil, from which plants grow to be gathered by people or eaten by game animals. The cycle of the seasons provides metaphors for the eras of their lives: springtime for children, summer for young adults, autumn for older adults, and winter for elders. Passages through these stages are celebrated in coming-of-age ceremonies, vision quests, marriages, and burial rites. The harmony and balance of creation are readily observed in their home environments and serve as models for their lives.

## *The Medicine Wheel*

Medicine Wheels are found throughout the western hemisphere, from the arctic to Antarctica. Much of the knowledge and understanding of these mysterious, circular rock formations has been lost. There are a variety of interpretations for what they represent, from ancient maps that identify the locations of events and phenomena to sacred philosophical constructs. To some tribes, they are considered sacred or of a powerful spiritual essence or purpose, showing the cycles of life, seasons of the year, and the relationship of an individual to the family/tribe and eventually the world/universe.

While there are many tribal variations, rocks are typically arranged on the ground in a circle or circles within circles, and sometimes they are separated into four quadrants. These can correspond to the four directions or the seasons, and they are often associated with the sacred colors of yellow, white, black, and red. Usually the circle in the center represents the Creator at the heart of all life. Medicine Wheels have a variety of purposes: for ceremonies, healing, marking burial sites, and communicating tribal boundaries or seasonal movements. "Medicine" refers to the spiritual power that is represented and invoked.

Despite the importance of the Medicine Wheel, I (Forrest) was not aware of it until my adult years. It has been said that the Utes were once quite familiar with the Medicine Wheel, but over time this knowledge has been lost. In any case, one summer when I was preparing for the challenges of the Sun Dance, as I lay down to rest, I was swept away by a vision. I found myself flying rapidly through the air, following the contours of hilly grasslands. Soon I was above a road winding through the high grasslands, with a huge mountain surrounded by other mountains looming in the background. The road straightened as I entered a flat valley and the pace quickened, becoming faster and faster. Just as I reached the base of the mountains, I woke up and lay in bed confused. Was I losing my mind? Would there be a message for me in the Sun Dance?

Nothing in the ceremony reminded me of the vision, but afterwards the Spirit told me to visit my oldest uncle, my grandmother's brother. I told him the story and he sat quietly, thinking for a while. "I know that vision," he said at last. "I've had that dream many times. The mountain represents your life. You're young, just starting to go up. Me, I'm older, most of the way up the mountain, but whenever I turn around to look back, I wake up."

Then the Spirit sent me to another uncle, and he had a different interpretation. "You're going up north to the grandfather country for some purpose," he said. "No, Uncle, I don't have any plans to travel." "Nephew, you'll be going there." Sure enough, several months later my job as tribal Education Director included an invitation to a Native Healing and Renewal Conference at the University of Lethbridge in Alberta, Canada. The focus of the teachings was the Medicine Wheel.

It is well known that Native people have been deeply traumatized by the horrors of our history with whites: deaths from violence and disease, the loss of our ancestral lands, our children being taken away to boarding schools, impoverishment, and incarceration. Widespread impacts of these traumas include the destruction of family ties, alcohol and drug abuse, loss of languages and ceremonies, chronic illness, and suicide. We have been a people out of balance for many generations, struggling to maintain our lives day by day. The purpose of the conference in Lethbridge was to help us use the ancient wisdom of the Medicine Wheel to return to harmony and balance. After what my uncles had told me, it was clear that I should pay attention.

## The Deadly Cycle

The cyclical nature of life represented in the concentric circles of the Medicine Wheel illustrates how different Native ways are from the dominant culture, which is much more linear. In the dominant world, life is viewed as a journey from A to B, with the goal justifying the means. This creates a human-centered (God-absent) model, in which people and resources are used to meet objectives like increasing profits. Faith becomes a Sunday morning activity rather than a guiding force and principle that is practiced daily. When individual "wants" take priority over community needs, it's a sign of arrogance, and Jesus's command to "love our neighbors as ourselves" is forgotten.[1]

---

1. Matt. 22:39.

Due to human limitations and failings (sin), arrogance opens the doors to greed. From March through December 2020, when COVID-19 brought a catastrophic economic time for so many Americans, our country "gained" fifty-six new billionaires, bringing the total to 659.[2] Although the pandemic was raging, the wealth of this tiny group increased by over $1 trillion, a heartbreaking example of greed. The dominant culture's goal orientation (on profits) and its emphasis on ends over means are ideally suited to generating wealth. Because shareholders and company executives are richly rewarded for their activities, greed becomes a driving force for decision-making.

When profits are the primary goal and "natural" resources are merely components of production, environmental destruction becomes inevitable. With managers under pressure to produce more and minimal regulatory oversight, there is no incentive to be concerned about impacts on the land or restoring degraded sites. The destruction accumulates over time, affecting local communities (often Natives or other people of color) and creating scarcity. For example, the diminishment and pollution of groundwater is a widespread problem, with major impacts on drinking water and food supplies for ordinary people. Multiplied by our many industries, these impacts amount to an assault on God's creation.

Worst of all, because the dominant culture's economic model generates so much wealth, it becomes comfortable for many leaders

---

2. Institute for Policy Studies, reported on NBC news online, December 30, 2020.

to overlook the human and environmental costs. A deadly cycle has been created in which arrogance leads to greed that causes destruction, and as profitability reinforces arrogance, the cycle becomes self-sustaining. The impact of this model on global climate change makes it truly deadly for all of us.

> *Dear Reader: All of us in contemporary American society participate in what we've described as a "deadly cycle." Seemingly ordinary actions such as driving a gas-powered vehicle have major impacts on our world. Middle-class people working to support their families (like the resource managers we mentioned) can get caught up in this troubling cycle. An important first step in making systemic changes is to recognize the workings of the system and the parts we play in it. Only then can we begin to appreciate a different way of seeing and doing things.*

## The Life-Giving Cycle

In Native traditions, every day is a gift from the Creator, and the natural response is gratitude. The blessings of each day are not meant to give us whatever we want, but to meet our deepest needs. This perspective is based on familiar, respectful relationships with the Creator and close connections with creation and our communities. When Native people speak of "all my relations", the term refers to the entire living earth, not just blood relatives. The Medicine Wheel pictures these relationships with concentric circles, all interrelated and mutually dependent, sharing joys and pain alike. A Native elder may mourn over a toxic waste dump as if a family member were critically ill, just as their heart will rejoice when a flock of birds flies north in the springtime.

If every day is a precious gift, then it is natural to give back generously to the Creator, the community, and all of creation. There are many Native people who don't hesitate to care for one another, and, for many, the only purpose for wealth is to give it away. This reinforces a sense of abundance in which hunts and harvests are celebrated and feasts are shared with others on every sort of occasion. Deep, caring relationships with creation make this bounty sustainable, because people take only what they need to live (versus whatever they think they want). A life-giving cycle is created as gratitude leads to generosity, promoting a sense of abundance that generates more gratitude, making it self-perpetuating. The Medicine Wheel can make this cycle visible and invite us to live our lives in balance and harmony.

Many of us see this Native Way as a model for deepening spirituality, reversing damage to creation and building stronger communities. We think it could transform any community, though embracing it raises major challenges: Native people (and others) will need to find healing to grow beyond trauma. People from the dominant culture will need to let go of control and think more of "we" than "me." Deeper connections with the Creator, creation, and community will be essential for both groups, and we will all need to be gracious to one another. The underlying foundation is nothing new. As Jesus said, "'You shall love the Lord your God with all your heart, and with all your soul, and with all your mind.'

This is the greatest and first commandment. And a second is like it: 'You shall love your neighbor as yourself.'"[3]

*As we'll describe in more detail, this Native Way is profoundly different from the dominant culture. It's not an alternative approach to achieving prosperity, but a fundamental reorientation of relationships. To get a glimpse of how it works, you might try putting a note on your bathroom mirror or above your coffeepot: "What am I thankful for today?" Would thinking about that several times a day make a difference in how you see the world?*

---

3. Matt. 22:37–39.

# 2 ▪ Gratitude

On the last morning of the Lethbridge conference that Forrest attended, four distinguished Native elders were present. Each of the conference participants could ask them any question about their lives. I (Forrest) said that I had experienced "déjà vu" and wondered what it meant. After a pause for my question to be translated and for the elders to reflect, a very stately and powerful-looking elder in full headdress, Ed Calf Roping, began to speak. He was a highly respected spiritual leader of the Blood (Blackfeet) tribe, and he spoke in his own language.

"Grandson," he said, "before we come to this world each of us is given a purpose by the Creator. The only way to know that you're on the right path . . . is when you experience déjà vu."

As we broke for lunch after that session, Charlie Crow Chief (another of the elders) leaned over to me. "Forrest," he said, "Come with me. I want to show you something." We got into his car and headed out of Lethbridge. As we drove up around a large hill, I started feeling energy and power. My heart was racing and I was breathing faster. I asked where we were going, but Charlie just smiled and kept on driving.

As we crested the hill, I saw several forked Sun Dance center posts located in various places in the meadow. I thanked him for bringing me to the ceremonial grounds and he replied, "I knew you were a Sun Dancer, and I wanted to show this to you." As I got out of the car, I looked beyond, shocked to see the rolling hills and big mountains from my vision before coming on this trip. Suddenly, I realized this indeed was the landscape I had seen in my vision of flying, and I understood why my uncle had said I would be coming to the grandfather country. Clearly, I was right where I was supposed to be, on the path to accomplishing my purpose.

## The Sun Dance

The Sun Dance is the most sacred ceremony of the Ute people; it is also celebrated by a number of other mountain/plains tribes, each in its own way. For us it is a time of fasting and sacrifice, with the dancers abstaining from food and water for three or more days. The thirst becomes so agonizing on hot summer afternoons that I've been reminded of the suffering of Jesus on the cross. When he found breath to voice the words, "I am thirsty," it connected Jesus with every person who has ever been in pain.[4] Sun Dancers embrace their fast on behalf of all our suffering people.

The Sun Dance takes place on ceremonial grounds, which are used only for that purpose. A circular corral is built each year for the dancers, with a huge forked tree trunk (usually a cottonwood) in the center representing the Creator or God the Father. Flags (one light- and one dark-colored) are usually attached to the top of each fork of the tree, representing the two opposing forces in

---

4. John 19:28.

the world (good/bad, light/dark, yin/yang). That central trunk is set firmly in the ground, with twelve poles (some say they represent the twelve apostles) radiating out from it and resting on an outer circle of posts. Leafy branches are cut for screening around the outside and are laid on the poles to provide some shade. The corral opens to the east to greet the sun during sunrise ceremonies. The dancers fill the perimeter of the corral with the Sun Dance chief (and sometimes a subchief) in the middle. The drum and singers are usually on the east side. Women elders are nearby, and some use willows and umbrellas for shade. At various times, men and women elders will get up and address the dancers, pray, and offer encouragement to them, usually in the Ute language.

Each dancer/person has a different interpretation of the Sun Dance. Personally, the Sun Dance has made me appreciate everything in life. My thirst and need for water become central and all-consuming. The ceremony is always held in the summer, when the hot afternoons suck up all my moisture. My body starts to hurt all over and it is hard to keep dancing. Even a slight breeze breaks up the smoldering heat and sets off a surge of gratitude. The coolness of evening relieves the most extreme thirst, but at our elevation of six thousand feet it can be bone-chilling cold at night, almost like winter. That makes the dancers eagerly anticipate the sunrise and the return of the day's warmth. Dancing makes me appreciate all the forces of nature: the sun and wind, heat and cold, and especially the life-giving water that forms most of our bodies.

Sunrise is the starting time for the dance and a sacred time for the Utes. The sunrise ceremony consists of the singing of four sacred songs while the dancers remain in their stalls, blowing eagle bone whistles to the beat of the drum. After the morning prayer, the chief usually gives a talk with instructions for the day. After the ceremony, there is a break to allow the dancers to prepare themselves. In some tribes, the dancers stand in one place. Our dancers go back and forth from their stalls to the center pole, blowing their whistles and dancing to the beat of the drum. Some family members and friends camp nearby throughout the dance, and others arrive before dawn to offer prayers and support. This gathering grows throughout the day, with people sitting in the hot sun to support the dancers and show solidarity and connection. By the third day I'm getting weak and desperate, almost ready to give up, and seeing my family and neighbors gathered outside the corral gives me strength. That is especially true of the elders: they know about suffering and their prayers are strong. Ultimately, it is the power of the dancer's spirit and faith in the Creator that gets them through the dance, for the dancers are pushed to their limits.

Like every Ute ceremony, the Sun Dance ends with a feast. This celebrates the community rising to another challenge, surviving a difficult test, and it honors the young men or women who have proved their courage and resilience. Elders lead prayers of thanksgiving and everyone enjoys the food, but as a dancer, there is no sweeter way to break my fast than by eating watermelon.

Throughout the Sun Dance, the chief and other elders speak to the dancers regularly, offering prayers and teachings and encouragement. My first dance was in Ignacio, Colorado, and I remember

Chief Eddy Box Sr. speaking of the "worldwide dimensions" of the dance. "We're not just dancing for ourselves and our families," he said, "but for all the tribes and all mankind and for every living thing." Recalling his wisdom makes me picture the Medicine Wheel, with its concentric circles radiating outward from the Creator to encompass the whole universe. It fills me with gratitude to know that I am part of all that is.

> *From time to time, many of us get glimpses of what's "beyond us." In powerful moments, worship can transcend its physical elements to a deeper, spiritual plane. Many people have that kind of experience in special places in creation. Athletes speak of being "in the zone" during intense parts of their games. These are all precious gifts in the midst of our busy lives, and it's important to pay attention to them.*

## The Sacredness of Creation

We have said that the familiar Native phrase "all my relations" refers to much more than our blood relatives. For us, creation is not "out there" somewhere, separate from the everyday world of people. All the earth is alive, every part of it, and we are related to all created things. We see the world as a web of connections: rivers and forests, mountains and deserts, mammals and birds, all infused with the divine spark and filled with the Spirit.

For decades, this Native perspective was patronized and rebuked by people from the dominant culture. However, recent scientific discoveries have illuminated the intricate interrelationships of living creatures and ecosystems. We celebrate the prophetic ecologist

Aldo Leopold, who in the 1940s challenged the prevailing mindset by writing, "We abuse land because we regard it as a commodity belonging to us. When we see land as a community to which we belong, we may begin to use it with love and respect."[5]

Christians have also dismissed Native theology as reflecting some kind of "nature worship." However, seeing God's creation as being infused with the divine and filled with the Spirit is perfectly orthodox. The first chapter of Paul's letter to the Romans tells us, "Ever since the creation of the world, (God's) eternal power and divine nature, invisible though they are, have been understood and seen through the things he has made. . . ."[6]

Paul's advice to look for God in creation makes perfect sense to traditional Native people, but we take that one step further. Beloved Ute Sun Dance Chief Jensen Jack said, "You go to church one day a week to thank God. Me—I pray and give thanks throughout the day. I wake up—thank you for the gift of this day. I drink water, eat food, give thanks again, Turgwayaq in Ute. When I see my friends and family, I give thanks again. I live my church every day, all through the day."[7] Being deeply connected with the Creator and creation is the foundation of our gratitude.

*People often think of prayer in rather formal terms. "Saying your prayers" commonly refers to words that are spoken before*

---

5. Aldo Leopold, *A Sand County Almanac*, 1949, Forward.
6. Rom. 1:20.
7. Oral communication with Forrest S. Cuch.

*meals and at bedtime. These are good foundations for developing a deeper practice of prayer. When we pause for a moment, are we thankful for a blessing or looking ahead to what comes next? Is our ongoing conversation with the Creator something to fit into our schedules, or does it unfold naturally? Little things like that can deepen our faith and make worship experiences even more meaningful.*

## Praying without Ceasing

Generations of Christians have struggled with the apostle Paul's insistence that we "Rejoice always, pray without ceasing, give thanks in all circumstances; for this is the will of God in Christ Jesus for you."[8] That sounds like a good idea, doesn't it? But we get swept away with our lives and have to make an effort to focus on prayer.

As we have just heard, that was different for Jensen Jack. Giving thanks throughout the day, every day, seemed perfectly natural for him. I (Forrest) had seen him a few times when I was growing up, but I didn't get to know him until I became the Education Director for my tribe. He began attending meetings to see what kind of person I was in promoting education. Did I believe that education should replace native culture (total assimilation, the colonialized approach) or could we promote both among our people (the adaptive/integrative approach)? Jensen was the Sun Dance chief back then, and all of us younger men looked up to him.

---

8. 1 Thess. 5:16–18.

He knew how much we were suffering and shared just the right combination of encouragement and discipline. His teachings were helpful, but most of all his presence and prayers set a spiritual tone for the whole group.

During this time, I was getting to know Jensen at a higher level. I think he approved of the way I did my job because I valued our traditional ways. One day, Jensen told me a powerful story that explained his life. Like many others, he'd been wild as a teenager, drinking and driving too fast and generally carrying on. One night he crashed his car and was badly injured, paralyzed from the neck down. He spent months in a hospital in Salt Lake City, utterly despondent. It seemed like he had ruined his life.

Besides being depressed, he was deeply humbled, heartbroken at squandering the gifts the Creator had given him. He began to pray throughout the day, begging forgiveness and promising to change his life. Very slowly, his condition began to improve. He was able to sit up in bed, and one day he slipped off the bed onto his feet, trying to gain his full balance. He looked at the door and wondered if he could get there on his own. Finally, he took the chance to reach for it, taking a step toward the door before falling. Initially the nurses were upset, afraid that he'd be hurt again, until he was pulled back onto the bed and one of the doctors discovered some muscle tone in his legs. They realized that soon he would be able to walk again.

When Jensen finally left the hospital and returned to his home in Tridell, at the foot of the Uintah Mountains on the north side of the reservation, the first thing he did was go out to the back of the house. He fell to his knees on the ground, thanking God for his healing and a new chance at life. While he was praying, he had a vision of a man standing before him in a transparent globe. The man, who had piercing eyes and a glowing heart, held up one hand with the other hand over his heart. (In the Roman Catholic tradition, this is referred to as the Sacred Heart.)

The man, who Jensen believed to be Jesus, communicated with him telepathically, saying "I heard your prayer and helped you. And in return, from this day forward, you will help your people." Soon after, Jensen went to his uncle Wallace Jack and asked to learn about the Sun Dance, and for many years following his uncle's death, Jensen served as Sun Dance chief. He taught many other young men like me, but most importantly, he showed us what a life of gratitude looked like. Jensen gave thanks daily for all things: sun, air, water, people. Everything.

An outsider to the reservation might not have identified Jensen Jack as a leader. He didn't have an office in the tribal headquarters or speak at public meetings. Patiently, in a quiet way, he helped to reinforce an atmosphere of prayerfulness among our people. The strong community support during the Sun Dance is a prominent example, but not the only one.

Jensen's practice of daily prayer is shared by many others, especially greeting the sunrise and giving thanks for the new day. That sets a pattern of seeing life as a gift and provides an entry point into the life-giving gratitude cycle. Showing respect for elders (who have walked many cycles of the seasons) fits alongside daily prayers, and it honors their role as spiritual models. Unlike the dominant culture, where older people are often dismissed and overlooked, Native elders are widely respected.

Public gatherings like tribal council meetings are opened with prayer, and big events like Pow Wows begin with flag ceremonies led by military veterans (especially elders). Ceremonies such as the Bear Dance (a dance that originated among the Utes), in sweat lodges or at burials, are steeped in traditional prayers. Hunters make offerings in gratitude for animals who have given their lives to feed the people, and the gathering of wild foods or herbs is accompanied by prayers and tobacco offerings.

When every day is a gift, the Creator a living presence, and creation a sacrament, gratitude is the most natural response. People from the dominant culture may not appreciate how important this is, but these relationships and spiritual practices are what separate traditional Native people from the arrogance so common in mainstream America. An attitude of gratitude doesn't just make people feel good—it draws us into the life-giving cycle that leads to generosity and abundance. And the Sun Dance reminds us that it can all be taken away, and we can be left with suffering, scarcity, starvation, and death.

*Some of the most prayerful people in our midst are not set apart as religious leaders. In fact, we may have encountered them many times before realizing how special they are. Do you know someone like this, perhaps an elder? Have you had a chance to talk with them and hear their story? In intergenerational settings, young people are blessed by the presence of mature spiritual models in their daily lives.*

# 3 ▪ Generosity

Though the two of us both grew up in the 1950s and 1960s, our relationships with extended family members were quite different. For me (Michael), they were people who sent Christmas cards and who we saw every few years. My daily experience at home was of Mom and Dad and my two sisters. A man from West Africa once tried to help me expand that picture. "Think of it this way," he said. "A cousin to you is like a brother or sister to me." At first I thought he was exaggerating, but he wasn't.

To me (Forrest), that makes perfect sense. In the Indian way, every family member around my parents' age was an aunt or uncle, and all the younger ones were my siblings. I had many grandparents, because every elder relative became one. Growing up on the reservation, most of them were close by, and it seemed like they all stayed at our house at one time or another.

We were fortunate to have a three-bedroom house, bigger than many of the government-built houses in those days. I barely remember any times when only our "immediate" family members were there. Aunts and uncles, cousins and grandparents—anyone who needed a place to stay or was visiting from out of town was welcome. Even though my mother worked full time, this never seemed like a burden to her. Welcoming relatives into her home wasn't just something she decided to do; it was a big part of who she was. My mom was grateful to have a house and was generous in sharing it. For me it meant there were always people in the living room talking and other kids to play with. It meant seeing women busy in the kitchen making and cleaning up big family meals. It meant that all the generations were together all the time. We didn't always get along perfectly, but what family does?

Of course, there were some relatives I felt closer to than others, and one was my grandfather (technically my great-uncle) Leonard LaRose. Uncle Leonard converted our place to a dairy farm by planting alfalfa and building a barn. Through those efforts, he provided fresh milk to the Fort Duchesne community. My folks had to watch him because he liked to drink alcohol. One time, he got drunk and wrecked his truck, spilling milk all over the place. For quite some time, the whole town was talking (and laughing) about that. I have precious memories of Uncle Leonard teaching me to whittle and encouraging me to take up the trumpet, which he played very well.

Another beloved grandfather was "Uncle Billy" Chapoose, or Wapenas. We used to sit for hours playing cards together, especially Quichuck (Ute for "I have it"), which was like Go Fish. No one knew exactly how old Wapenas was, but after his death in the 1970s, the grandmothers agreed that he was over 100. That meant he was born right after the Civil War and was with the families in the Uintah band who were moved from the rich habitat around Utah Lake (south of Salt Lake City) to the high sagebrush desert of our reservation.

Being banished from the only place they had ever known must have been traumatic, but they stayed deeply connected with the

Creator and always took care of one another. They shared everything from food to caring for the young and old to providing lodging and other needs. Possessions were held in common, and if anyone had food, then everyone ate. Sharing wasn't just something they did; it was who they were, their way of life. Faithfulness and generosity were among their most important survival skills.

What a contrast that makes to the individualism of the dominant culture. While there is a sense of community there, it rests on a foundation of "survival of the fittest." For white people, it often seems that a gift is what a wealthy person gives out of what is left over. For Native people every day is a gift from the Creator; gratitude and generosity are the natural responses. This isn't just among the Utes. Anthropologist Carlos Barrio has identified generosity as the number-one shared value of Native people throughout the Western Hemisphere.[9]

Recently a young, white woman asked me, "What's contributing to the world's problems?" While today's troubles are deep and complex, my answer was simple: we have lost our connection with the Creator. People have grown too comfortable and complacent, putting their energy into financial "security" and maintaining the status quo. Seeing each day as a gift is only possible if we are deeply connected with the Creator and all creation. That is the key to appreciating our blessings and to living generous and compassionate lives.

---

9. Carlos Barrio, *The Book of Destiny*.

*Families come in all shapes and sizes, and to kids growing up, whatever is familiar feels "normal." Each type of family system has its own values, which are passed on in subtle and often unspoken ways. As adults, we have opportunities (if we take them) to reflect on the values of our upbringing, either claiming or modifying them.*

*Gratitude and generosity are inherited values, which we learn about as we're growing up. The feeling that there's "never enough" does not necessarily reflect what someone outside the family might observe. It could indicate a sense of diminished status, compared with other community members. Conversely, people with few material resources often feel blessed and see cooperation and generosity as basic survival strategies.*

## Living Generously Today

Despite massive cultural disruptions since we were forced onto the reservation, generosity is still woven into the fabric of the Ute Indian Tribe. Feasting is an integral part of all our ceremonies, and everyone is welcome at the table. Not only do the Bear Dance and Sun Dance conclude with community feasts, but those Mondays are tribal holidays so everyone can attend.

Coming together after the deaths of beloved family members and longtime friends is a critical part of our resilience as a people. Wakes in family homes are usually crowded, with women keeping vigil with the body in the living room, men gathered around a fire in the yard and lots of food in the kitchen. Traditional prayers continue through the night, during the funeral service and at the cemetery, including appropriate honoring songs being sung, after which everyone gathers for a feast. Whether the food is provided by the family or the tribe or is offered as pot luck, it's a generous expression of hospitality.

Spiritual gatherings in sweat lodges or churches are typically followed by sharing food. Episcopalians sometimes joke about coffee hour being the "second sacrament," but lunch at St. Elizabeth's in Whiterocks, Utah, is a well-established part of our Sunday routine. The same holds true for a variety of family gatherings (holidays, birthday parties, baby showers, graduations, and so on), at which sharing food plays an important part. It's a concrete, tangible way to honor the gifts of the Creator and our connections with one another. It certainly was that way with Jesus, who caused a stir by attending too many dinner parties and by eating with the wrong sort of people.[10]

Caring for young and old people is another ongoing expression of generosity. Sadly, the traumas inherited from past generations and today's widespread temptations have had a major impact on younger Native parents. Alcoholism, drug addiction, and domestic violence have put children at risk, but family members almost always step in to keep them safe and secure. Because virtually every family home is intergenerational, it's natural for many grandparents, aunts, and uncles to generously provide the physical and emotional security that children need to thrive.

---

10. Matt. 11:19

Unfortunately, that kind of response has not always carried over to the care and companionship needed by many elders. Where once their status as home owners or designated residents gave them opportunities to invite younger people into their households, an increasing number of tribal elders are living alone. As in the dominant culture, their isolation has practical, emotional, and health-related effects, which lower their quality of life. That is especially disappointing because the principle of respecting elders remains well accepted in tribal communities.

It's been heartbreaking for me (Michael) to realize that what seemed like generous impulses of Christians in the past have left a terrible legacy with Native people. The efforts by churches to provide education through boarding schools were disastrous failures, leading in many cases to horrifying child abuse or death. While we have not heard of that occurring at the boarding school in Whiterocks (which was operated by St. Elizabeth's and which many of our older members attended), this colonialized approach was devastating to the transmission of the Ute language to younger generations. That stemmed from the church's lack of understanding of intergenerational households and an arrogant disregard for the importance of their native language to the cultural identity and practices of the Utes. Today we are seeking to make amends by respecting Native leaders and supporting them in reaching out to the children and teenagers of the reservation community.

Ironically, though many or most Utes don't identify with the church, their Native way of living embodies Christian values like generosity. At the Last Supper, Jesus commanded his disciples to continue the practice of feasting, which he loved so well: "Do this in remembrance of me."[11] The great commandment to love God and neighbor closely parallels foundational Native teachings about the relationships among the Creator, creation, and the community.[12] The generous sharing of living spaces with children would have been appreciated by Jesus, who said "just as you did it to one of the least of these who are members of my family, you did it to me."[13] And though economic systems based on sharing resources are often dismissed with a derogatory label ("socialism"), the traditional Native way of living together closely resembles the practices of early Christians, who shared their resources.[14] Though generosity may sometimes seem foreign to the culture of individualism, it's entirely consistent with Christian faith and Native practices.

*We all hope that the values others see in us (and in our families) reflect our best intentions. Because it's hard to view ourselves objectively, it can be helpful to notice people in our communities whose values we appreciate. What sets them apart from others? Which of their values caught our attention? If possible, it might be interesting to hear their story and learn more about how they came to be the people they are today.*

---

11. Luke 22:19.
12. Matt. 22:37–39.
13. Matt. 25:40.
14. Acts 4:32.

## *The Legacy of Wapenas*

Leaving a legacy seems like a practice of the dominant culture, in which a financially successful person makes arrangements to transfer their wealth to future generations. Uncle Billy Chapoose (Wapenas) was not known to be rich, but the gift of land he was able to leave to his family was incredibly precious. By all accounts, Uncle Billy was a deeply spiritual man. He was rooted and grounded in the traditions and ceremonies of his people. Not only did he speak Ute, but he knew many of the "old words" endowed with special power. He was a spiritual leader, a prominent singer, and fire keeper for the Sun Dance.

As with Jensen Jack, an outsider might not have recognized what an important leader Uncle Billy was. Traditionally the Utes didn't have permanent positions of authority. Instead, we relied on a more flexible, situational approach to leadership. Wapenas's work with the Bureau of Indian Affairs police grew out of this model, focusing on reconciliation, healing, and what today we would call restorative justice. For Uncle Billy, there was no clear line between spirituality and law enforcement. He was what was considered back then a true "peace officer."

In his work, Uncle Billy witnessed a relentless assault on our traditional culture. The Dawes Act, passed by Congress in 1887, subdivided the land the Utes (and other tribal people) had always held in common into individual family "allotments."[15] Then the

---

15. Forrest S. Cuch, ed., *A History of Utah's American Indians*.

Homestead Act of 1905 opened "excess" land on the reservation to homesteaders, who flocked into the area. Wapenas watched as the Ute Indian Tribe and its members lost more than two-thirds of their land to "private" (white) ownership. While the settlers saw building farms and farming communities as signs of progress, many or most of them also assumed (and rightly so) that the Utes would be easy pickings on the land market. Uncle Billy saw many of his friends and neighbors trading or selling their land for a pittance: a little cash or a gun or a few bottles of alcohol. He was determined to make whatever impact he could to reverse this process.

The starting point for Wapenas was to hold on to his family's allotments, including a parcel on the Whiterocks Road. Because he saw the land as a gift, he treated it with reverence. In a simple outbuilding, he and his friends gathered with their drum, practicing songs (prayers) for the Bear Dance, Sun Dance, Pow Wow, and other occasions.[16] The land, the prayers, and his relationship with the Creator were inseparable. In the midst of the extreme disruption of Ute culture, that place remained an oasis of the sacred.

Looking toward the future, Uncle Billy could have returned his parcel to the tribe. Instead, he sought to instill in his family a sense of the sacredness of the land and its importance as a legacy for their spiritual future. Eventually it came to me (Forrest), and though my career took me away from the reservation, it kept a

---

16. Discussions with Geneva Chimburas.

strong hold on my heart. I visited regularly and slowly built the house I live in today. This land has become a sanctuary, and caring for it is one of my greatest joys.

Time has brought me personal growth and healing, and the land played a big part in that. Now that I am retired, I get to share the gifts that have come to me. When people visit my horses or camp on the land, when foxes or sandhill cranes or elk pass by, when my friends join together in the sweat lodge, I feel Uncle Billy's spirit with us. Thanks to his foresight and generosity, when my son and grandchildren are here, I know that the cycles of creation are continuing.

*It says a lot about mainstream American culture that we assume the word "legacy" refers to money. While cash is very visible and practical, we receive other kinds of inheritances from our families. Creative pursuits, the love of being outdoors, cooking and baking, mechanical and building skills are among many other examples. These are gifts that "keep on giving," often received from our ancestors and hopefully passed on to the next generations. It's easy to take legacies like these for granted; we need to cultivate the personal stories which remind us how much we have to be thankful for.*

# 4 ▪ Abundance

The story of Moses leading the people of Israel through the Red Sea to freedom still resonates powerfully more than thirty centuries later. It's easy to forget that the Promised Land was not waiting for them on the other side, however. Once the Israelites had celebrated their great victory, they set off on a long, dangerous journey through the desert wilderness. The conditions were very challenging, and they did a great deal of complaining. Naturally, all their problems seemed to be Moses's fault. "Would that we had died by the hand of the LORD in the land of Egypt, when we sat by the meat pots and ate bread to the full, for you have brought us out into this wilderness to kill this whole assembly with hunger."[17] The Lord heard their complaint and responded generously. Bread (manna) rained down from heaven every morning, and in the evening, quails came up and covered the camp.

Miraculous as this sounds, it was not enough for those "stiff-necked people."[18] "We remember the fish we ate in Egypt that cost nothing, the cucumbers, the melons, the leeks, the onions, and the garlic; but now our strength is dried up, and there is nothing at all but this manna to look at."[19]

---

17. Exod. 16:3.
18. Exod. 33:3.
19. Num. 11:5.

Surviving in the wilderness isn't easy; clearly the Israelites would have been much worse off without the Lord's intervention. Their food supply was dependable, and gathering manna and quail every day couldn't have been easier. Even so, what they had didn't *feel* abundant. For one thing, the Lord was giving them the staples they needed to survive, rather than the array of fresh foods they wanted. In addition, when they tried to store up manna, it spoiled.[20] On their wilderness journey, faith in the Lord's providence was the only source of security.

## The Utes' Journeys

Ironically, the journeys of my (Forrest's) people to the Uintah and Ouray Ute Reservation were the exact opposite of the Israelites. Our original territories were versions of the Promised Land! The Uintah bands had lived in the rich valleys south of Salt Lake City, with Utah Lake teeming with fish, plenty of grass for their horses, and the mountains nearby for gathering wild foods and hunting. The Whiteriver and Uncompahgre bands lived in beautiful Colorado River valleys, with buffalo and other big game all around them, trout in the streams, and plenty of food to gather. Gratitude to the Creator came naturally amid such abundance.

What a shock it was for our people to be overrun by settlers and miners; to see treaties broken and to be forcibly displaced from our homelands to an arid, barren reservation. The conditions

---

20. Exod. 16:20

here were much more challenging, and the promised rations were often hijacked by outlaws or sold by unscrupulous agents. Fortunately, our ancestors were keen students of nature, learning (by necessity) what they needed to know to survive in a new and unfamiliar place. Sharing whatever they had helped everyone, and they eventually raised a few cattle and sheep to supplement other food sources.

Most of all, they depended on praying to the Creator. Even if they didn't have much, they never forgot to give thanks for it. Their gratitude and generosity never failed.

> *Today's Americans come from a multitude of backgrounds; virtually all of our families lived in another part of the world six hundred years ago. Some chose to come here for new opportunities; some desperately sought a place where they could survive; some were enslaved and sold to landowners. Millions of people indigenous to North America still live here today.*
>
> *Knowing something about the history of our own families and the Native people of our current homelands can help us understand the complex and often troubled relationships which bind us together. Mutual respect can only arise when we know each other's stories. One place where most of us can begin to show that respect is by making regular land acknowledgements, such as this one: "St. Elizabeth's Episcopal Church occupies and operates upon the ancestral and traditional lands of the Ute Indian Tribe."*

## *What Is Abundance?*

A hundred and fifty years later, our traditional values continue to provide the spiritual foundation for the Ute people. Since coming to the reservation, we've never had much in material terms, but as we saw with the Israelites, abundance is a relative concept. Three very different people have been the greatest influences on my life, and each of them taught me about abundance.

My mother, Josephine LaRose Cuch, was educated (from the age of eight to eighteen) at Sherman Indian School in Riverside, California. Not only did she graduate from high school, but she completed a two-year business school program. She returned home to become the secretary to the Agency Superintendent, and years later she became the indispensable Office Manager at the Indian Health Service clinic in Fort Duchesne. Besides overseeing all the office functions, she interpreted for patients who only spoke Ute and drove people to specialist appointments in Salt Lake City. She was a very dedicated employee who knew the people well and was able to serve their needs.

My mother made it clear to me that abundance is not a matter of possessions, but a consequence of gratitude. "Appreciate what you have," she said many times, "and you'll always have more."

Dr. Mack Gift was a professor at Westminster College in Salt Lake City, who became a lifelong friend. He recognized the negative impact that racism was having, and he helped me to overcome it by learning to love myself. He convinced me that I was projecting my own self-hate onto other people, which would destroy me.

Conversely, he taught me that loving myself enables me to love others. He jokingly grumbled that he'd been a perfectly good atheist before meeting me, but "too many unexpected things happen around Forrest." Dr. Gift taught me that abundance is a consequence of generosity. "When you give, you get," he liked to say, and he lived his life that way.

You've already gotten to know Jensen Jack, so his influence on my life shouldn't be a surprise. Jensen showed me that abundance is a consequence of regular and continuous prayer. "Give thanks for every little thing, all day long," he would say, and his words rang with authenticity.

*If we pause to reflect on the formative experiences of our lives, most of us will remember people who made a positive impact on us. Not only can that make us thankful, but we may be able to reach out and share the blessing. Being contacted by a former student, athlete, or employee can really make someone's day, and ours too. As we gain life experience, perhaps we'll have a chance to help someone along their way.*

### Homecoming

After leaving my position as the Education Director for the Ute Indian Tribe, I (Forrest) was blessed with remarkable opportunities to be of service to other Native communities. I was appointed to the position of planner for my first wife's tribe, the Wampanoag Tribe of Aquinnah, located on Martha's Vineyard Island, off the southern coast of Massachusetts. The tribe had been granted federal recognition in 1987 and was awarded four hundred acres of undeveloped land. Soon after I began that work, I learned that Martha's Vineyard was one of the most highly regulated places in the entire United States. I prayed for help and it arrived in the name of the late Dr. Chuck Harris, a Harvard University Professor of Landscape and Design. Under Dr. Harris's guidance, we developed a master land use plan using a process that is called "charette." We were encouraged to invite some white neighbors initially opposed to our efforts to join us in the planning process, which eventually led to the highly successful construction of an access road, then a tribal office building and housing on those undeveloped lands.

In 1997, I was appointed Director of the Division of Indian Affairs for the state of Utah. I found my work with the Utah tribes very rewarding and fulfilling and served in that position for more than thirteen years, under four different governors. Although I enjoyed positive relationships with my colleagues, I experienced many frustrations with state policymakers and some legislators. Many times, I was expected to be subservient, and I was actually told not to advocate for my people! In 2011, I was relieved of my duties, and it was time to go home.

Partly, the draw I felt to return was from the people, my relatives and others I'd known for so many years. It was also the magnetic pull of our family's land on Whiterocks Road, so carefully preserved and generously given into my care by Wapenas, my Uncle Billy Chapoose. I had visited whenever I could and always got a great feeling from being on the land, but there was no house to live in, and I couldn't imagine how one could be built.

While living in Salt Lake City, my wife and I had bought a comfortable condo at the mouth of Emigration Canyon, which suited our needs well. I had a good job and qualified for a mortgage loan, which gave us buying power in the housing market. That's not how it works on the reservation. The family parcel that I inherited is on federal trust land, meaning that it could only be sold to the tribe. Mortgage lenders and title companies wanted nothing to do with an arrangement like that, so I was on my own in terms of building a house. Or at least it seemed like I was.

One day I found myself at a workshop, doing a creative visualization exercise. I made a collage from magazine photographs, with a picture of a Native man and a little girl (who I visualized as my future granddaughter) in the center. Next to them was a nice, two-story house, with a beautiful garden filled with vegetables. Beside that was a gleaming, white pickup truck. There was also what looked like a restaurant, with a display of delicious food. Without consciously planning, I'd been led by the Spirit to create an image of my dreams, and I became very excited about it!

That motivated me to visit a business that modeled different kinds of houses. I was only looking for a one-story rambler, thinking that was all we could afford. I found a simple plan that would do just fine, but my wife encouraged me to look at some other models. We walked into a two-story home in which the whole first floor was open, with a high vaulted ceiling, which featured elongated windows for better views. My wife fell in love with it, but I knew we could not afford it, so I refused to entertain it as a possibility for a future home.

The next day, I recalled my wife's son, who is a building contractor, saying that it is cheaper to build a second floor than to build a larger base. I called him to explore this further. He told me that he could have his architect draw up the plans and do a cost estimate for me. He soon got back to me, and my Spirit told me to go with his ideas.

## Lessons Learned

The good news is that it all worked out; I'm sitting at my desk looking at that view while I write. The other part is that it took years to complete the house, and several times the project was on the brink of failing. I could tell the Spirit was at work, but my faithfulness in prayer was sorely tested. Numerous times I had to ask myself, is this just something I want, or do I truly need it? If it's the latter, what responsibilities am I assuming along the way?

I did not have the money for this home to begin with, and because we couldn't secure a mortgage, I chose to "build as you go." At times, the money came in by dribs and drabs from all sorts of unexpected sources, until it didn't and the project was stalled for two years. When I called the builder about getting started again, he sighed and said he'd been thinking about getting in touch. This was certainly no plum job, but it had captured his heart and he wanted to finish.

Looking back, in the discouraging times I was forced to remember what I'd learned about abundance. My mother always said, "Appreciate what you have, and you'll have more." Was I grateful for the blessings in my life, or had I become obsessed with my goal? Dr. Gift taught me, "When you give, you get." Was I still being generous in sharing my gifts?

Most powerfully, I remembered Jensen Jack's story of returning home from months in the hospital and falling to his knees in grateful prayer. I realized that building a house wasn't about me at all; I'm just a temporary caretaker. At its heart this is a sanctuary, gifted into my care by Uncle Billy and held in trust for my grandchildren. It's a place where visitors can camp and people in need of healing can visit my horses or pray in the sweat lodge. The soil brings forth vegetables for the kitchen and bales of hay for the horses. This land is home to deer and elk, sandhill cranes and a host of other birds, small critters and an occasional moose. The house is also a refuge for me and my family.

Most importantly, I was ultimately blessed with a beautiful little granddaughter as I had visualized! I had already been blessed with a beautiful grandson, but I wanted a granddaughter to complete my life's fulfilled picture. I'm so fortunate to have grandchildren, whom I enjoy immensely.

Having been blessed so bountifully, my heart aches for all those who are homeless, with no families, struggling to find the barest shelter to get through the night. The Creator's gifts are abundant, enough for everyone if we'll just take what we really need and share the rest. And remember to give thanks to God, every minute of every day.

> *What makes a dream come true? With Forrest's house there seem to have been a number of elements. He felt called to return home and had received the legacy of his family's land. He was both determined and patient, making progress whenever he could, but also willing to wait for the next opportunity to arise. Recognizing that the house was really a gift for future generations was critical; it helped him align with the Spirit and trust in the process. Whatever we may be called to build, our lives will require a similar combination of determination and devotion. When God is working through us, we'll always have enough of what we really need.*

# 5 ▪ Abundance in Action

Pat Sanger had a challenging job, and nothing helped her unwind after work more than walking on the beach. As an Advanced Psychiatric Registered Nurse, she cared for a number of African-American children living in poverty. "Teachers referred them to the clinic where I was working, thinking they had attention deficit disorder," she said. "When I evaluated them, I realized they were acting out as a result of having been traumatized."[21] During her beach walks, the outlines of a therapeutic and preventive program began to take shape in her mind: verbal and artistic self-expression . . . mentoring by trusted adults . . . confidence-building . . . physical exercise and shared meals . . . Sanger thought she might call the program "Arts-Kids."

Before she could put these ideas into practice, Pat ended up moving to Park City, Utah. Arts-Kids started up in those comfortable, mountainous surroundings and developed a following, but her vision wasn't complete. Pat still wondered what the impact might be in a chronically traumatized community, where young people are subject to bullying and racism, addiction, school difficulties, early pregnancy, legal troubles, and suicide.

---

21. Private communication from Pat Drewry Sanger, September 17, 2020.

## *Arts-Kids in Whiterocks*

A few years later, Sanger joined a group from St. Luke's Episcopal Church in Park City in driving out to the Ute Reservation to meet with members of St. Elizabeth's. She quickly realized that she had found the kind of community her program had been designed for, as well as people who were committed to serving the youth. "I was sitting with Emmy Cesspooch, a young Ute woman, at lunch and I told her about Arts-Kids," she said. "By the time lunch was over, we agreed that Arts-Kids would be a program which would address many needs on the Ute Reservation."[22]

It turned out that Pat had also found a dynamic partner in The Rev. Sue Duffield of St. Elizabeth's. Sue drew upon her extensive network of relationships to organize the program, connecting with adult family members "who were happy their children had somewhere safe and fun to go every week." One teenage boy told her, "We wish we could come here every afternoon; then we wouldn't get in trouble hanging out on the streets."[23] Meanwhile, Pat provided training to Ginny Chimburas and other leaders, who became the heart of the program. Generous financial support from the local Rotary Club, St. Luke's and the Episcopal Diocese of Utah paid the operating expenses, and Arts-Kids, Whiterocks was on its way.

St. Elizabeth's had (as we have said) a troubled legacy of working with young people on the Ute reservation. This new program brought the hope that the church could move beyond the boarding

---

22. Ibid.
23. Email from The Rev. Sue Duffield, February 28, 2021.

school era by addressing some of the community's deepest concerns. From the beginning the kids and teenagers loved Arts-Kids, and it drew appreciation from church elders, families on the reservation, and the Business Committee (the Tribal Council), all of whom saw the young people as their number-one priority. Supporting this effort became the primary mission of the church, echoing Jesus's decree to his disciples to "Let the little children come to me and do not hinder them; for to such belongs the kingdom of heaven."[24]

> *There's a visualization exercise that, though somewhat unnerving, can be helpful in seeing our congregations through new eyes. Imagine (God forbid) that a tornado touched down in the night and destroyed the church buildings, with no injuries. Who, besides the members, would notice that they were gone and miss them?*
>
> *For most Episcopalians and many other Christians, Sunday worship forms the central axis of church life. Like it or not, during the pandemic we've learned that worship is possible without gathering in our buildings. The same is true for Bible study and adult education, though it's not quite the same on Zoom. Food pantries and soup kitchens are different; however, some level of presence is required. The same seems to be true of 12-step meetings, and it certainly is for our expressive arts program. These missions engage the community in ways that complement Sunday worship, fulfilling our call to follow Jesus in lives of service.*

24. Matt. 19:14.

*If we know the most important God-given purposes of our churches, we can focus our investments of time and treasure on them. When the possibility was raised at St. Elizabeth's of starting a youth group, to supplement Arts-Kids with faith formation, we didn't hesitate to commit ourselves. "We need to do this," Forrest said, "and we will." When our mission is clear, we know the Spirit will help us find a way to carry it out.*

## *Abundance*

Without a doubt, Arts-Kids brought an abundance of fun to everyone involved. The kids and teens enjoyed being with their friends after school, free of the academic demands and social challenges they experienced every day. They loved the art work, responding to new ideas and interesting materials, and the hour sitting together at the art tables passed quickly. Outdoor play was popular, both spontaneously and through organized games, and the day always ended by sharing a healthy meal, with plenty of leftovers. The same kids who rode quietly in the vans after school talked boisterously on the way home.

The key to the growth of our Arts-Kids program was local leadership. SueAnn Cotonuts, a mainstay of the church and a longtime Head Start teacher, excelled in the role of Classroom Coordinator. She, Ginny, and other Native women, who knew the kids and were connected with the families, formed the hub of the relationships that helped the program grow. Young adult Becca Gardner described what it was like to become the leader of the teen group: "At first it was kind of scary, being in charge of the teenagers and making sure things got done. Once we got into a routine, it started being fun for all of us." The group grew steadily, mentoring developed naturally, and a sense of abundance resulted from the program leaders generously sharing their gifts.

Alongside the regular adult leaders, Native guest artists introduced the young people to the Ute heritage and shared their own stories as artists. For example, Mariah Cuch helped them make cutouts of tipis, portraying what their family looks like (on the inside of the cutout) and what their neighborhood looks like (on the outside). Storyteller and filmmaker Larry Cesspooch brought traditional Ute tales to life and invited the youth to draw their own story boards. Artist and substance abuse counselor Michelle Chapoose led them through a multimedia project illustrating "The Ocean of My Emotions." Rose Cuch taught them to bead medallions using age-appropriate methods, and LeRoy Cesspooch led circle dances accompanied by traditional songs and drumming. Roberta Windchief's "ledger art" project took them back to the early reservation days, when the only paper available for drawing was from discarded ledger books. Champion hoop-dancer Charles Denny introduced them to his art, and Adrian Eagle Hawk and Geraldina Selestewa helped them try out familiar pow wow dances. What an abundance of opportunities for hands-on learning and just plain fun!

Our generous financial supporters continued to make it possible to offer all of this at no cost to the families, and we were blessed by a series of grants from Newfield Exploration Company. An oil company—deeply engaged with the community and blessed by the presence of tribal member Elton Blackhair—Newfield provided a model for energy companies to give back generously.[25] We were fortunate to become aware of their interest, but once we did our approach was simple: keep telling the story of a small, local church focused on serving the community's needs. We knew that with additional support we could do more, and we were grateful to be able to demonstrate that.

We were also blessed by the support of artist and grant-writer Lola Beatlebrox, who greatly improved the focus and presentation of our requests. From her experience she pointed us toward opportunities for proposals, helping us apply for and receive a number of grants from foundations, businesses, and service organizations. A generous gift came from St. Elizabeth's, which donated the proceeds of our Paycheck Protection Plan loan once it was forgiven and turned into a grant. It was exciting for the church to give away this money for such a good cause. We could have put it in the bank or found some other way to spend it, but we took seriously the gospel teaching in the Sermon on the Mount: "But seek first the kingdom of God and his righteousness, and all these things (your necessities) will be added to you."[26] Since it was clear that

---

25. Sadly, the late Elton Blackhair died of complications of COVID-19 on December 21, 2020. A devoted husband and father, and a Sun Dancer, Blackhair served as Newfield's liaison with the Ute Indian Tribe and was instrumental in securing funding for Arts-Kids.
26. Matt. 6:33.

caring for the community's children and youth (the "little ones" to whom the kingdom belongs) is our top priority, investing our time and money for their benefit was an obvious choice.

After Pat Sanger retired and moved out of state, the time came for us to separate organizationally from Arts-Kids, Inc. We held a contest among the teenagers to choose a new name and Maria Alanis came up with the winning idea: Art Empowers. Preparing to publish an issue of our newsletter, I (Michael) called the house on a Saturday afternoon and asked if she could write the new name on paper and pose for a picture with it. After her years in Arts-Kids, it shouldn't have been a surprise that she came to church the next day with a gorgeous poster, with colorful lettering and hand prints over a dream catcher background. The abundance of her creativity expressed and embodied the significance of the new name.

> *We hope everyone starting out with grant writing will find a mentor as helpful as Lola has been for us. You'll want to look across your state for someone who knows someone like that, and keep telling your story. "Big Box" stores, utility companies, and other large corporations often make charitable contributions. Put together a one-page handout with colorful photos to illustrate the impact of your program. Take advantage of any personal connections, and follow up with a letter and another copy of your handout. Save the letter in your computer to make writing the next one easier, and keep track of who has been contacted and when. Express your gratitude for every little favor, and remember that this is not about you, but the people you serve.*

## *The Lunch Makers*

The COVID-19 pandemic was looming on the horizon as Art Empowers' spring series began in 2020. As it turned out, the local schools closed down soon after our first program day, and we did too. But what a day it was! Young people seemed to appear from everywhere, and as we sat in the opening Talking Circle, kids were still being dropped off and finding seats.

It was the kind of spring day when the memories of winter begin to fade away, so everyone was in a good mood. Our familiar program rituals flowed along as we introduced ourselves and checked in, then moved to the art tables to make medallions for the new talking stick. It was a great time for outdoor games and playing with friends, and our dinner together was relaxed and satisfying. Little did we know that we wouldn't be together in person again for more than a year.

At first, the pandemic seemed to the youth like an early summer vacation, an unexpected chance to stay up late and sleep in and generally take it easy. As the days turned into weeks, very few of them seemed to be engaged with their online classes. It also became clear there was something they missed about school besides seeing their friends: the lunches. The school district was still providing them, but only at the school sites. None of the reservation towns have their own elementary or middle school, and with no buses running, the lunches were out of reach for many of the young people.

The pandemic is unique, but it's sad to say that hungry people are nothing new. After a big gathering by the Sea of Galilee, highlighted by Jesus's inspired preaching, the people began to grow restless. " . . . the day is now over;" the disciples told their master, "send the crowds away to go into the villages and buy food for themselves." But Jesus said, "They need not go away; you give them something to eat."[27]

That sounds simple, but it was too much for the disciples. They depended on Jesus to multiply the loaves and fishes, but in Whiterocks we witnessed a different kind of miracle. We knew the kids who were missing lunch; we'd given them rides home from Art Empowers many times. Becca and her high-school-age nieces Pepper, Maria, and Nehemiah Alanis (all part of the same household) jumped right in. They texted a few families to confirm the need and went into town, but grocery shopping was nerve-wracking. "We'd told people we'd make the lunches," Becca said, "and we didn't want to let anyone down. But when we got to Walmart, the shelves were almost empty. We had to go to five grocery stories and still barely got enough supplies."

To avoid drawing a crowd to the parish hall, they decided to drop off the lunches at the family homes. SueAnn (the mother and grandmother of the lunch makers) helped them make the deliveries. The word began to spread to other households, and at every home they discovered brothers and sisters, grandmothers and aunties who also wanted lunches. Serving twenty people each day quickly grew to fifty and seventy-five, but the team never faltered. The teenagers could have been sleeping late, but as Nehemiah said,

---

27. Matt. 14:15–16.

"We love helping our community and our people as much as we can." Maria added, "It was fun making the lunches. We got to see the smiles on people's faces when we dropped them off."

From handling the credit card receipts, I (Michael) knew that the expenses were adding up. The next time our Bishop's Committee (church board) met by conference call, we talked about the cost of the lunches. Fortunately, Becca and Pepper are board members, so we got to hear their firsthand reports. "We can't stop now," they told us. "These people need our help." Becca and her nieces were claiming leadership, and the strong backing they received from the church encouraged them to carry on. They'd been shaped by the most basic Christian moral teaching: " . . . You shall love your neighbor as yourself."[28]

Fortunately, we'd been careful with our finances and had plenty of savings to cover these mission-related expenses. We didn't have to draw on that, however, because after a newsletter article was written about the lunch makers, donations came pouring in. Church members gave special gifts, a local business made a generous donation, and one of our members started calling his friends, inviting them to help. Before long we'd received over two thousand dollars, plenty of funds to pay for our grocery costs. We were deeply grateful, and Nehemiah wrote on a thank-you card, "We all appreciate your donation, because we get to continue what we love doing." Maria observed that, "This has made me a better leader. I've realized there are things I can accomplish that help

---

28. Matt. 22:39.

others and make me a better person." As Forrest's mentor Dr. Gift said, "When you give, you get."

One part of the story's happy ending is that the school district recognized the need and began distributing lunches at the community center in Whiterocks. By then the lunch makers were so excited about this work that they decided to continue once a week. There's a saying in the church that "money follows mission," which certainly was true in this case. By the time school started (online) in the fall, about two thousand meals had been provided, and we'd received another two thousand dollars in donations to cover the costs.

We've continued to tell this story, because there are important lessons in it for all of us. Being grateful for the food they have gave the lunch makers compassion for the ones who were struggling. Once our members and friends heard about the project, their generosity seemed to be contagious. Not only were the expenses taken care of, but the three teenagers became aware that they have the power to change the world. That's the power of the gospel at work.

> It's sad but true: in every community in our wealthy nation, there are people whose basic needs are not being met. Often they're not immediately visible, but the more we connect with people, the better we'll see what's needed. The best way to respond is by starting small and following up faithfully. If a young adult and three teenagers from a little congregation can make a big difference, you can too.

# 6 ▪ The Generosity of the Elders

A very sacred part of the hoop of life has been broken: the relationship between the elders and the youth. In previous chapters, I (Forrest) talked about my great uncles who came to serve as my grandfathers. I was blessed by these men because they enriched my life in so many deep, subtle, and meaningful ways. But this kind of relationship is at risk in current-day society; so many demands have been placed on families, even in our tribal community, that the elders have become marginalized, separated from the younger generations.

In the traditional days of my people, before coming to the reservation, it was the elders who raised the children. The parents were busy obtaining the necessities of daily life. The men usually participated in governance and planned hunting, war, and trading excursions. Women secured food by picking berries, gathering herbs and nuts, and by digging roots. They also skinned and butchered meat, as well as curing the hides to make clothing and lodging (tipis).

Over the ages, the elders developed unique ways of raising children. Rather than demanding obedience, they did that experientially, coaching the young people to make their own decisions. The elders taught responsibility early on for actions and consequences. For example, rather than ordering a child to get down from a tree, an elder might explain the possibilities and let them make their own choice. A child might climb numerous trees, and if he or she fell, they'd recognize the consequences of their own decision.

This traditional role of elders played an important part in the birth of Arts-Kids in Whiterocks. Respected church leaders like Madeleine Martinez and Ginny Chimburas were driving forces, participating in the activities, but most importantly, giving the congregation's blessing to this new program. They generously turned the focus away from their own generation to the needs of the young people, clarifying the mission of the church in the process. By being present they shared their wisdom and caring, letting the young people know how precious they are.

## The Prodigal Father

The Parable of the Prodigal Son has the wrong name. "Prodigal" means wastefully extravagant, which does describe the younger son when he was buying wine for his friends. However, the gospel story[29] should really be called the Parable of the Prodigal Father.

The dad in the story was not prodigal in the usual sense of the word. He was careful with money and saved up inheritances for *both* his sons. With lots of help from his older son, he kept the farm in good, well-care-for condition. He could be counted on to be there when he was needed, even if he had to wait for years.

---

29. Luke 15:11–32.

The father was prodigal with love and forgiveness. Even though the younger son had left the hardest work for his brother, squandered his inheritance, and humiliated the family, his dad never gave up on him. When the son returned after being away for years, his father forgave him before he even asked, hugging him and giving him a fancy robe, ready to throw a party to celebrate. None of that was deserved; all of it was extravagant.

Only an elder can be that generous. Only after we've tried and (sometimes) failed, made good choices and bad ones, will we have the humility to show such outrageous love and forgiveness. Only when the end of our lives comes closer can we pour out all that's best in us. The older brother didn't understand because he wasn't an elder. Not yet, anyway.

> *This story from the Gospel of Luke offers many possibilities for personal connections. We've all known someone like the dissolute younger brother (not us, of course), right? What about the long-suffering older brother, always faithful in his work? As we grow older, do we aspire to be more like the father, or is he enabling his son's bad behavior?*
>
> *Those of us in the baby boomer generation comprise the largest group of older people our country has ever known. What do we need to learn, and how do we need to grow, to reclaim the status of elders?*

## The Whiterocks Elders

The generosity of elders at St. Elizabeth's extends far beyond Art Empowers; it's a central feature of the life of our congregation.

For a small Episcopal church, we're blessed by the presence of all the generations, much like the Utes' tradition of intergenerational families. A few years ago, a Native woman in her thirties joined the church, coming from an evangelical background. I (Michael) could see this was quite an adjustment, and after a couple of months I asked how she was getting along. "I love it!" she said without hesitating. "I've heard about St. Elizabeth's for a long time, but I didn't know you had the elders."

Reflecting on our congregational life, it seems like they're (quietly) everywhere. When I attend a wake on the night before a funeral, I'll frequently see one of our elder women sitting in the living room with the family. More than once I've watched Ginger Ridley circulate through the crowd at a funeral reception, chatting with young and old, offering encouragement. She reminds me of the advice my spiritual director gave me about hospital visits: "Don't just try to do something," he said. "Sit there and talk!"[30] An hour after finishing our Sunday lunch, a group of women will still be gathered around a table in delighted conversation, slipping in and out of Ute and laughing frequently.

It's no surprise to be watching the opening flag ceremony at the pow wow and notice one of our elder men like Adelbert Tavashutz or Leo Tapoof among the other veterans, carrying a flag or the eagle staff. Leo is a faithful spiritual leader, equally likely to be offering traditional prayers in Ute at the Sun Dance or on a special

---

30. Deepest thanks to The Rev. Dr. Francis Geddes.

occasion in church or at a Veterans Day ceremony. I treasure the memory of going with Leo to gather water for baptisms at a sacred spring; he offered tobacco and a moving prayer before we touched the water. He spent an hour one day drawing a diagram to illustrate the connections between the Sun Dance and our Christian faith. Forrest also serves as a bridge between these traditions, leading sweat lodge ceremonies alongside his writing and teaching.

Sometimes the most transcendent moments in worship are very simple. On her ninety-fifth birthday, Leo offered a traditional blessing for our beloved elder Jane Thompsen. He laid hands on her head and spoke movingly in Ute, with "Jesus Christ" included several times. One of our members, who understood every word, told me how beautiful the blessing had been.

Jane lived in the Uintah Basin (the original reservation territory, more or less) for almost fifty years. She had a huge impact on the community, starting a school for special needs students, spearheading the creation of a Family Support Center for families in crisis, tirelessly raising money to build a Juvenile Justice Center and advocating for a "Receiving Center" to separate juveniles from adult prisoners. Her lifetime of service was inspired by her strong Protestant faith, and she never forgave the Utah church leaders for closing the little Presbyterian church in the Basin. After that she joined St. Elizabeth's along with some of her "children," adults she'd supported in in the process of getting clean and sober.

One day Jane invited me to go to the jail with her. She was past ninety at the time and had been leading Saturday Bible studies at the county jail for ten years. I'd visited there before and knew the security routine, but being with Jane was entirely different. As she walked slowly through the waiting room, a deputy came running to unlock the doors for her. Once inside she seemed to know everyone and greeted people by name. "What are you doing here?" she scolded one inmate. "You promised you'd never come back!" The woman just smiled sheepishly and gave Jane a big hug.

Bible study was well-attended, and after the scripture readings Jane delivered what must have been a version of her usual message: Jesus is with you and his grace surrounds us, but you'd better get your act together and start making better choices. No one wanted to leave when she finished; they all treasured their time with her.

In the last week of her life, I got to enjoy a relaxed visit with Jane. One of her sons and his family were there; we sat around a toasty wood stove on a winter day, talking and enjoying each other's company. Then in a quiet moment Jane suddenly said, "I hate just sitting around. There's so much more left to do!" Whatever image we may have of an "active senior" was way too small for Jane.

*Retirement isn't what it used to be. Especially after the pandemic, many seniors have little interest in sitting around home, passing the time. With gifts and skills cultivated over a lifetime, we could be contributing to the greater good. Many of us need to keep on earning to live comfortably.*

*Churches and nonprofits have an unprecedented opportunity to draw on this talented group in carrying out our missions. While it wouldn't involve earning money, making a difference for people in need can be deeply satisfying. Step One is taking this generation seriously. Get to know people and find out what (and how much of it) they love to do. Building in opportunities to connect with friends will make getting involved even more attractive.*

*Step Two is inventing every possible excuse to bring seniors together with younger single people and families. Plan meals and outings, arrange technical support for those struggling with their phones and computers, organize intergenerational outreach projects (for example, Christmas caroling followed by hot chocolate). Be creative, and don't write off the members of any generation by making assumptions about them.*

## The Future of the Church

Imagine this: St. Elizabeth's 2021 Annual Meeting was the highlight of everyone's day! To be as inclusive as possible, we did it by telephone conference call, and eight people (mostly elders) joined in. Because this was a new process, at first they'd barely say their names. Then one of the women said something funny and everyone joined in, talking and laughing. It really was a shame to interrupt that by starting the meeting. After the usual vicar's report and discussion of our finances (which were doing fine despite the pandemic), Forrest spoke about his pride in our church family for staying connected when we couldn't get together in person. "Despite the sadness of illness and deaths," he said, "our mutual support and prayer really help. The historical strength and resilience of the Utes came through again when we needed it."

Then I asked if there were any comments or questions, and a long silence followed. Somehow, I managed to keep waiting, and finally one of the women hesitantly began to speak. She talked about the impact aging was having on her place in the family, and this resonated with the others. As Forrest said later, "It's ironic that the elders of today love their young so much, that they choose to be placed in nursing homes, because they do not want to be a burden to their younger family members." The Ute Indian Tribe has programs for elders but no dedicated residence, probably because of the tradition of intergenerational households. Sadly, as we said earlier, that's working better for children than it is when elders are in need.

Looking at America's dominant culture, spiritual teacher Michael Meade observed that "a person cannot become an elder by simply becoming older. . . . People either wise up to who they are at the core of their soul or else tend to slip into narrow, egocentric patterns."[31] What we see at St. Elizabeth's is affirming in that regard. Despite the historical trauma present throughout their lives, our elders seem to be approaching their later years with grace and humility, gratitude and faith. Seeking no personal benefit, they generously offer themselves in service to others. "Whenever someone's dying," one of them told me, "the family always wants me to come and sit with them." Simply by being present, they manifest the Spirit of Christ.

---

31. Michael Meade, Mosaic Voices, Facebook, May 7, 2020.

St. Elizabeth's is blessed by the abundance of gifts we receive from the elders. I pray (and I think) that our younger members are being shaped and formed by the time we all spend together. In this disjointed, twenty-first century world, a crucial role may be emerging for the church. Amid so much division and alienation, we're becoming the new intergenerational household. Could this be a key to the revival of the post-pandemic church?

# 7 ▪ Trauma and Gratitude

For people in Centennial, Colorado, December 13, 2013 was a day of horror. At a little after noon, a student at Arapahoe High School entered the school library with a shotgun he'd just purchased, seeking revenge on his debate coach. He randomly shot another student (who died of her wounds), set off a Molotov cocktail and then took his own life. The entire rampage lasted only eighty seconds, but its reverberations can still be felt.

Arapahoe is a high-performing school in a comfortable, white suburban neighborhood south of Denver. It would be tempting to say things like that don't happen there, but sadly, they had. Thirteen years earlier, in a neighborhood only a few miles away, two heavily-armed young men at Columbine High School killed twelve of their classmates and one teacher. Eighteen months before the Arapahoe shootings, a gunman had entered a movie theater in another Denver suburb during a Batman premiere (attended by many high school students) and killed twelve people, wounding fifty-eight others. The things that "don't happen in a place like this" had turned into a recurring nightmare.

St. Timothy's Episcopal Church, where I (Michael) was serving in 2013, is two blocks down the street from Arapahoe High School. We had a large youth group and knew dozens of students at the school. A text from our youth leader ("get down here") brought me to the youth room, where a crisis was raging. Her phone was literally blowing up with texts from young people at Arapahoe and every other high school. No one knew that the violence had already finished. In fact, we had every reason to be picturing an armed rampage through the halls with many more victims.

The school was locked down in terror for hours. A young woman well-known to us texted that she was hiding with others in a closet, before her phone went dead, leaving us imagining the worst. A young man we knew was returning from lunch when the shooting broke out; he ran for his life, expecting a bullet at any moment. Later we found out that his brother had to tackle a teacher who thought it was all a drill, to prevent him from opening the classroom door.

The police responded very quickly, but they had no way of ruling out the presence of another, hidden shooter. After a couple of hours with no further violence, the students were marched out of the building one class at a time, in single file with their hands over their heads. After being searched, they were reunited with their families at a nearby elementary school, with many tearful hugs.

It wasn't just the students, staff, and family members from Arapahoe who were traumatized; shock waves reverberated through the whole community. Counselors were there to listen, candlelight prayer vigils were held, and the governor spoke at a huge memorial service for the young woman who died. Our youth group got together regularly, including a day when they made sack lunches and gave them away to people on the street in downtown Denver. (One of the men receiving a lunch told the young people, "We've been praying for you.") The Arapahoe library was gutted and rebuilt, a beautiful memorial was created on the grounds, but before all that work was finished, the students and teachers went back to school.

## Resiliency

Almost a year later, I got a call from a counselor at the high school. To respond to the long-term effects of the trauma from the shootings, they were planning a program on resiliency. Their hope was to hold it nearby but not on the school grounds, and we were happy to offer our large sanctuary. Over two hundred students, teachers, and parents attended the session, which was led by Dr. Bryan Sexton of Duke University. Dr. Sexton told us about his extensive studies of resiliency, which have documented the effectiveness of a program he calls "The Three Good Things."[32]

"We are hardwired to remember the negative," he wrote. "Our best response is to turn up the volume on the positive." Dr. Sexton has a simple method for doing that. "Just before sleep, ask yourself: 'What are three things that went well today, and what was my role in making them happen?'"[33] Because writing them down produces the best results, Dr. Sexton suggested keeping a gratitude journal,

---

32. Dr. Bryan Sexton, February 10, 2014, www.midmichigan .org/3goodthings
33. Ibid.

which "makes people happier, less depressed, and sleep better."[34] He said that doing this every night for two weeks makes an impact that can be measured months later. Focusing on what we're thankful for is simple, but it can change our lives.

## Trauma

All of us experience trauma, the deeply disturbing experiences that can have a variety of negative impacts on our lives. It was clear in Centennial that the effects of repeated traumas are compounded. I noticed that people who were in Colorado when the Columbine shootings occurred were triggered by the violence at Arapahoe High School in ways that others were not. Common sense tells us that a person who has survived a terrible car accident will probably react very strongly if their car skids on the ice. To some degree, chronic trauma becomes a part of who we are.

Imagine if the people of Centennial were part of a social group whose youth had been shot and killed every generation for a hundred years or more. Those traumas would multiply, triggering reactions so widespread that their individual origins couldn't be traced. This is what is known as historical or intergenerational trauma, which Forrest has described as "cumulative emotional and psychological wounding from massive group trauma across generations."[35] Sadly, intergenerational trauma is deeply embedded

---

34. Dr. Bryan Sexton, St. Timothy's program handout, December 4, 2014.
35. Forrest S. Cuch, Episcopal Diocese of Utah Doctrine of Discovery Initiative, PowerPoint, February 5, 2020.

among Native people and African-Americans, as well as with many other groups worldwide.

Is Pat Sanger's vision for Arts-Kids more clear in this context? The African-American children she had worked with had a lot in common with the young people on the Ute reservation. The elements of the therapeutic and preventive program she designed were meant to help release deeply embedded trauma: verbal and artistic self-expression, mentoring by trusted adults, confidence-building, physical exercise, and shared meals. Along with these approaches, it seems possible that keeping a gratitude journal might be helpful for people of all ages in this community. As we've seen, gratitude is a traditional Ute value, the entry point into the life-giving cycle that leads to generosity and abundance. It was Sun Dance Chief Jensen Jack who said, "I give thanks throughout the day for everything: sun, air, water, people. Everything." His daily spiritual practice aligns perfectly with Dr. Sexton's research.

*Before serving on the Ute reservation, it was hard for me (Michael) to comprehend historical, intergenerational trauma. I'd gotten a glimpse of it among African-American people, but my experiences in Whiterocks and conversations with Forrest brought it to life. What would have seemed like unbearable tragedies in my middle-class roots, were the latest expressions of an unrelenting pattern of trauma for the Utes, stretching back almost two hundred years. Remembering how my white neighbors in Colorado reacted to the violence at Arapahoe*

*High School (on top of the Columbine and the Aurora Theater shootings) helped me empathize with Native people.*

*Having my heart broken open by being present as a pastor on the reservation has helped me begin to appreciate the resilience of the Ute community. If it's hard for mainstream Americans to focus on gratitude, what about someone in circumstances like Jensen Jack's? Slowly, it's been dawning on me that the Native Way's life-giving practices will be essential for all of us, in facing the challenges of the twenty-first century. From our social/political divisions to the devastating impacts of climate change, we'll be sorely tested in the years to come. We all need to cultivate resilience, and Native people (among others) may be the best teachers.*

*Forrest, who has known personal trauma and has spent much of his life crossing boundaries, emphasizes our shared humanity in his presence and teachings. There's no substitute for spending time together, but Americans today are thoroughly separated by race and income, especially in where we live. The greatest diversity I've experienced has come through the Episcopal Church, in congregations with many West African and Native members. For that I feel so much gratitude, which is the key that unlocks the life-giving cycle leading to generosity and abundance and ever-deepening gratitude.*

## Cultivating Gratitude

I (Michael) began keeping a gratitude journal after the workshop on resiliency, though over the years my entries have been irregular.

Since coming to Whiterocks I've written many pages of lists of people and events I'm thankful for. This seems like a good opportunity to share some of those anecdotes, which hopefully will be helpful for the St. Elizabeth's community, our generous partners in Utah and beyond, and even for the wider church. Certainly there have been plenty of challenges and problems over the years, which I'm sure you can imagine. Still, I wonder: What would it be like for more of us to keep track of the people and events we're thankful for? Those reminders could help to balance out the negative focus that's so prevalent in today's world.

*These are some of the people and events at St. Elizabeth's we're thankful for over the past few years:*

In a spirited discussion at a Bishop's Committee meeting a couple of years ago, we decided to invite the whole reservation community to a holiday meal in our parish hall. It was a daunting commitment, and we wondered whether we should pay to have food catered, so we'd be sure to have enough. After thinking a moment, Becca said, "No, we can do this with home-cooked food." Our worries were for naught, as the parish hall was packed, with most seats filling up more than once, and there was food left over at the end.

One year we had decided to focus our summer camp program around putting up and using our big tipi. A couple of days before camp started, the man who planned to help us was called out of town, so we talked after church about what we could do. "No problem," said longtime member Lena Duncan. "I'll ask my brother." Baldwin came on Monday morning with his nephew and enthralled the young people with family stories about camping in a tipi when he was a kid. He got them involved in every aspect of putting it up, which none of them had done before, and we all felt a strong sense of connection with this Ute tradition.

Mary Coe's late husband Elmon had come to Whiterocks during the summers of the 1930s to help his family run the local trading post, which some of our elders remember. Despite moving to the East Coast, the connection remained strong for her, and when a windfall came from family oil leases in our area, she donated the money to the church. It helped to pay for thirty pies, which at her suggestion we delivered to local families when the pandemic forced us to cancel our holiday meal, as well as for the purchase of a laptop for a new college student.

Grade schoolers Aveah and Caley love Art Empowers and also attend church almost every Sunday, with one of their great-grandmothers. They started bringing bags of coins, which were placed in a special offering container and used only for outreach. The girls have donated hundreds of dollars over the years, which were matched by the Bishop's Committee and paid for backpacks of canned food for the summer campers, turkeys for two years' Holiday Meals, repairs for an elder couple's car, and Walmart gift cards for families at Christmas.

During the pandemic we've stayed connected in a number of ways, including using Facebook to share our writing and prayer services. On four occasions our posts have gone modestly viral, with hundreds of views or likes for spiritual writings about COVID-19 (shared in New Zealand by a Maori friend), announcements of the Lunch Makers' project, special prayers for a Native woman who was murdered in Nevada (shared by our friends on the Paiute reservation), and our Christmas Eve services.

After I (Michael) had been serving at St. Elizabeth's for a year, it seemed like time for a fall stewardship campaign. Since there hadn't been one the year before, I made some simple pledge cards and showed them to one of the elders. "Indians don't sign papers like that," he said, so I put them away. It turned out that those cards were not necessary in this congregation.

Watching leaders rise up in the congregation is one of my greatest joys as a priest. Forrest Cuch is a wonderful Bishop's Warden (Board President), providing wisdom and guidance for all our decisions, as well as being a powerful writer and speaker. We can't imagine the children's section of Art Empowers without the gifted leadership of SueAnn Cotonuts and her relationships with the families and kids. She and her family fill multiple pews every Sunday, and SueAnn also leads morning prayer when my wife and I are gone. Becca Gardner has become a dynamic and skilled teen leader and Bishop's Committee (B.C.) member, spearheading projects like the holiday meal and the

Lunch Makers. Teenager Pepper Alanis is also a B.C. member, as well as being our principal Chalice Minister, leading occasional prayer services and serving as the Bishop's Chaplain when he visits. Adam Twiss has returned to the church with passion and served as a Case Manager for the Ute Tribe's Alcohol Substance Abuse Prevention Program, as well as helping to lead Sunday music. All of these people generously offer their gifts, inspired by their faith in Jesus and by being part of St. Elizabeth's church family.

Preparing to preach at the funeral of a young adult, I was meditating on the passage from Isaiah 25 about the Lord preparing a feast on the sacred mountain. Suddenly I heard Forrest's voice in my head, saying "The Utes are mountain people." With that I left the pearly gates behind and focused my message on the high Uintah mountains as an image of heaven, with all our departed loved ones gathered together, feasting. That really spoke to the people attending the funeral.

When one of our elders contracted COVID-19, we all began to pray for her recovery. We rejoiced when she went home from the local hospital, but then she was airlifted to Utah Valley Hospital in Provo and our prayers intensified. That whole cycle was repeated, and we kept on praying. The elders always want to know about pastoral news, whether it's good or bad, so they can pray for people in need. We rejoiced on the Sunday when she and her family returned to church.

We've taken three trips with teenagers to Salt Lake City, staying for several days at the Episcopal Church Center and exploring the city: going to an urban pow wow, strolling around a mall, working in a food pantry, spending silent time in St. Mark's Cathedral, visiting the Native Voices exhibit at the Natural History Museum and the Aquarium, shopping at the huge Harmon's grocery store, volunteering at the YWCA, splashing at the water park, watching the Pioneer Day parade, and seeing fireworks from the steps of the State Capitol. Becca leads these adventures, always bringing art materials and journals for reflecting on the experiences.

Mountains and Deserts is a regional coalition of Episcopal Indigenous Ministries, which hadn't gotten together for ten years, until we gathered in Salt Lake in 2019. People came from churches in Idaho, Arizona, Nevada, and Utah, and the whole time together felt like a family reunion. Everyone had inspiring stories to share, and the worship was wonderful. The teenagers joined the adults to lead us in the Talking Circle process they use every week at Art Empowers, before setting out for their own activities.

St. Elizabeth's receives very generous financial support from the Diocese of Utah, for our operating expenses and to help us maintain our facilities. Bishop Hayashi has been a special friend to the congregation, always encouraging us and sharing powerful personal stories in his sermons. One year we hosted the youth of the diocese for a weekend, with service work, outdoor adventures, games, a campfire, and heartfelt worship. The young people were moved by Leo Tapoof's sweetgrass blessing at the Sunday service, and our elders loved having the sanctuary filled with youth.

Joining together for lunch after worship is a basic part of our Sunday routine. Sometimes we struggle a bit to arrange for the food to be made, but it always works out in the end. The elders eat first, the conversation never lags, and sometimes we'll do something special afterwards, like sitting down together for a Lenten journaling session or hearing one of Forrest's presentations.

Amanda Jacobs came to St. Elizabeth's as one of Jane Thompsen's "children," struggling to begin a new chapter in her life. Amanda was very shy in church at first, but gradually she discovered how much the older Native women care for her. Celebrating Amanda's kids' baptisms and watching her faith grow have been high points for all of us.

Baptisms are always wonderful, especially for kids from Art Empowers. They've often come on their own, which shows how strongly they're drawn to the church. We don't have a Sunday School, but the young people who attend make pictures on 5x7 note cards, present them at the altar, and see them displayed around the room. Some of the water for baptisms comes from the tribe's sacred spring, Big Springs, as well as from the sacred waters of Pyramid Lake in Nevada, given to us by our dear friend The Rev. Reynelda James.

Winter Talk is the annual national gathering for Episcopal Indigenous Ministries. Joining that big crowd was a little intimidating at first, but now Forrest has served on the Advisory Council, Becca and Pepper have friends who greet them, and Carleen Kurip and Adam have joined in on Zoom. It's great to renew old friendships and make new ones, and we were thrilled when our missioner, The Rev. Dr. Bradley Hauff, came to Whiterocks to visit. Being part of this larger community is an inspiration and comfort for us, and we're deeply grateful for the leadership of our Presiding Bishop, The Most Rev. Michael Curry. Along with the guidance of The Rev. Sue Duffield, it was a talk by Bishop Curry at the 2016 Dakota Access Pipeline (DAPL) water protest in North Dakota that inspired Forrest to join the Episcopal Church, which would have pleased his late mother, Josephine LaRose Cuch, and The Rev. Quentin F. Kolb, a mentor.

# Epilogue

It is clear to us as we write that there is a powerful force/purpose driving this book. We find ourselves living in one of the most dangerous times in recent human history. Our country is deeply divided, teetering on the brink of civil war. We're facing our own self-destruction due to climate change (which we have triggered due to our willful neglect) and wanton pollution and destruction of Mother Earth. We have access to wondrous technology, the likes of which had never been seen or imagined before this time. We also have access to weaponry that can kill and destroy our planet ten times over. We sometimes boast of these accomplishments, but we have lost touch with the responsibility that possessing such technology and power brings. We are locked in a deadly cycle, far too concerned about money and our material well-being. We focus more on our rights than our responsibilities: responsibilities to our neighbors, our communities, and our Mother Earth. Will we continue to walk blindly into the future with little concern for God's will for us?

We believe it's possible to reconnect with our Creator through practicing gratitude and generosity. It is time to put forth a genuine devotion to God first and our neighbors, including all of God's creation. It is time to restore the values and beliefs that have given us strength and brought us into this time, a time that can be cherished if we can take the best of technology and use it for good.

It is time to heal and repair the damage that trauma has caused in all of our lives over past generations. It is time to forgive ourselves and each other and to pledge to our Savior Jesus Christ to follow his ways into and beyond the twenty-first century. May the Lord be with us always! Turgwayaq (in Ute, thank you).

CPSIA information can be obtained
at www.ICGtesting.com
Printed in the USA
JSHW051052131121
20395JS00001B/30